CEREMONY and other poems

CEREMONY

AND OTHER POEMS

Richard Wilbur

New York
HARCOURT, BRACE AND COMPANY

The following poems appeared originally in *The New Yorker:* "In the Elegy Season," "Juggler," "The Sirens," "Years-End," "Grasse: The Olive Trees," and "Clearness." Other poems have appeared in *American Letters, Botteghe Oscure, Harvard Advocate, Hopkins Review, Inventario, Imagi, Partisan Review, Poetry, Poetry New York, Quarterly Review of Literature, Tiger's Eye, Virginia Quarterly,* and *Wake.*

TO F.O.M.

CONTENTS

CEREMONY and other poems

THEN

Then when the ample season
Warmed us, waned and went,
We gave to the leaves no graves,
To the robin gone no name,
Nor thought at the birds' return
Of their sourceless dim descent,
And we read no loss in the leaf,
But a freshness ever the same.

The leaf first learned of years
One not forgotten fall;
Of lineage now, and loss
These latter singers tell,
Of a year when birds now still
Were all one choiring call
Till the unreturning leaves
Imperishably fell.

CONJURATION

Backtrack of sea, the baywater goes; flats
Bubble in sunlight, running with herringbone streams;
Sea-lettuce lies in oily mats
On sand mislaid; stranded
Are slug, stone, and shell, as dreams
Drain into morning shine, and the cheat is ended.

Oh, it was blue, the too amenable sea.
We heard of pearls in the dark and wished to dive.
But here in this snail-shell see, see
The crab-legs waggle; where,
If altered now, and yet alive,
Did softness get these bitter claws to wear?

As curtains from a fatal window blown
The sea's receding fingers terribly tell
Of strangest things together grown;
All join, and in the furl
Of waters, blind in muck and shell,
Pursue their slow paludal games. O pearl,

Rise, rise and brighten, wear clear air, and in
Your natal cloudiness receive the sun;
Hang among single stars, and twin
My double deep; O tides,
Return a truer blue, make one
The sky's blue speech, and what the sea confides.

"A WORLD WITHOUT OBJECTS
IS A SENSIBLE EMPTINESS"

The tall camels of the spirit
Steer for their deserts, passing the last groves loud
With the sawmill shrill of the locust, to the whole honey
    of the arid
    Sun. They are slow, proud,

    And move with a stilted stride
    To the land of sheer horizon, hunting Traherne's
Sensible emptiness, there where the brain's lantern-slide
    Revels in vast returns.

    O connoisseurs of thirst,
    Beasts of my soul who long to learn to drink
Of pure mirage, those prosperous islands are accurst
    That shimmer on the brink

    Of absence; auras, lustres,
    And all shinings need to be shaped and borne.
Think of those painted saints, capped by the early masters
    With bright, jauntily-worn

    Aureate plates, or even
    Merry-go-round rings. Turn, O turn
From the fine sleights of the sand, from the long empty oven
    Where flames in flamings burn

    Back to the trees arrayed
    In bursts of glare, to the halo-dialing run
Of the country creeks, and the hills' bracken tiaras made
    Gold in the sunken sun,

    Wisely watch for the sight
    Of the supernova burgeoning over the barn,
Lampshine blurred in the steam of beasts, the spirit's right
    Oasis, light incarnate.

THE PARDON

My dog lay dead five days without a grave
In the thick of summer, hid in a clump of pine
And a jungle of grass and honeysuckle-vine.
I who had loved him while he kept alive

Went only close enough to where he was
To sniff the heavy honeysuckle-smell
Twined with another odor heavier still
And hear the flies' intolerable buzz.

Well, I was ten and very much afraid.
In my kind world the dead were out of range
And I could not forgive the sad or strange
In beast or man. My father took the spade

And buried him. Last night I saw the grass
Slowly divide (it was the same scene
But now it glowed a fierce and mortal green)
And saw the dog emerging. I confess

I felt afraid again, but still he came
In the carnal sun, clothed in a hymn of flies,
And death was breeding in his lively eyes.
I started in to cry and call his name,

Asking forgiveness of his tongueless head.
. . . I dreamt the past was never past redeeming:
But whether this was false or honest dreaming
I beg death's pardon now. And mourn the dead.

PART OF A LETTER

Easy as cove-water rustles its pebbles and shells
In the slosh, spread, seethe, and the backsliding
Wallop and tuck of the wave, and just that cheerful,
    Tables and earth were riding

Back and forth in the minting shades of the trees.
There were whiffs of anise, a clear clinking
Of coins and glasses, a still crepitant sound
    Of the earth in the garden drinking

The late rain. Rousing again, the wind
Was swashing the shadows in relay races
Of sun-spangles over the hands and clothes
    And the drinkers' dazzled faces,

So that when somebody spoke, and asked the question
Comment s'appelle cet arbre-là?
A girl had gold on her tongue, and gave this answer:
    Ça, c'est l'acacia.

LA ROSE DES VENTS

POET:
    The hardest headlands
Gravel down,
The seas abrade
What coasts we know,
And all our maps
In azure drown,
Forewarning us
To rise and go.

And we shall dwell
On the rose of the winds,
Which is the isle
Of every sea,
Surviving there
The tinted lands
Which could not last
Our constancy.

LADY:
    That roving wave
Where Venus rose
Glints in the floods
Of farthest thought;
What beauty there
In image goes
Dissolves in other
And is not.

There are some shores
Still left to find
Whose broken rocks
Will last the hour;
Forsake those roses
Of the mind
And tend the true,
The mortal flower.

8

EPISTEMOLOGY

I

Kick at the rock, Sam Johnson, break your bones:
But cloudy, cloudy is the stuff of stones.

II

We milk the cow of the world, and as we do
We whisper in her ear, "You are not true."

CASTLES AND DISTANCES

I

From blackhearted water colder
Than Cain's blood, and aching with ice, from a gunmetal bay
No one would dream of drowning in, rises
The walrus: head hunched from the oxen shoulder,
The serious face made for surprises
Looks with a thick dismay

At the camera lens which takes
Him in, and takes him back to cities, to volleys of laughter
In film palaces, just as another, brought
By Jonas Poole to England for the sakes
Of James First and his court, was thought
Most strange, and died soon after.

So strangeness gently steels
Us, and curiosity kills, keeping us cool to go
Sail with the hunters unseen to the walrus rock
And stand behind their slaughter: which of us feels
The harpoon's hurt, and the huge shock
When the blood jumps to flow?

Oh, it is hunters alone
Regret the beastly pain, it is they who love the foe
That quarries out their force, and every arrow
Is feathered soft with wishes to atone;
Even the surest sword in sorrow
Bleeds for its spoiling blow.

Sometimes, as one can see
Carved at Amboise in a high relief, on the lintel stone
Of the castle chapel, hunters have strangely come

To a mild close of the chase, bending the knee
  Instead of the bow, struck sweetly dumb
    To see from the brow bone

  Of the hounded stag a cross
Grown, and the eyes clear with grace. Perfectly still
  Are the cruising dogs as well, their paws aground
  In a white hush of lichen. Beds of moss
    Spread, and the clearing wreathes around
    The dear suspense of will.

  But looking higher now
To the chapel steeple, see among points and spines of the
      updrawn
  Vanishing godbound stone, ringing its sped
  Thrust as a target tatters, a round row
    Of real antlers taken from dead
    Deer. The hunt goes on.

II

  They built well who made
Those palaces of hunting lords, the grounds planned
  As ruled reaches, always with a view
  Down tapered aisles of trees at last to fade
    In the world's mass. The lords so knew
    Of land beyond their land.

  If, at Versailles, outdrawn
By the stairs or the still canals, by the gradual shrink of an urn
  Or the thousand fountains, a king gave back his gaze
  To the ample balanced windows vantaged on
    The clearness near, and the far haze,
    He learned he must return.

Seen from a palace stair
The wilderness was distance; difference; it spoke
    In the strong king's mind for mercy, while to the weak,
    To the weary of choice, it told of havens where
        The Sabbath stayed, and all were meek,
        And justice known a joke.

        Some cast their crowns away
And went to live in the distance. There there was nothing
            seemed
    Remotely strange to them, their innocence
    Shone in the special features of the prey
        They would not harm. The dread expense
        Of golden times they dreamed

        Was that their kingdoms fell
The deeper into tyranny, the more they stole
    Through Ardens out to Eden isles apart,
    Seeking a shore, or shelter of some spell
        Where harmlessly the hidden heart
        Might hold creation whole.

        When to his solitude
The world became as island mists, then Prospero,
    Pardoning all, and pardoned, yet aware
    The full forgiveness cannot come, renewed
        His reign, bidding the boat prepare
        From mysteries to go

        Toward masteries less sheer,
And Duke again, did rights and mercies, risking wrong,
    Found advocates and enemies, and found
    His bounded empire good, where he could hear
        Below his walls the baying hound
        And the loud hunting-song.

MUSEUM PIECE

The good gray guardians of art
Patrol the halls on spongy shoes,
Impartially protective, though
Perhaps suspicious of Toulouse.

Here dozes one against the wall,
Disposed upon a funeral chair.
A Degas dancer pirouettes
Upon the parting of his hair.

See how she spins! The grace is there,
But strain as well is plain to see.
Degas loved the two together:
Beauty joined to energy.

Edgar Degas purchased once
A fine El Greco, which he kept
Against the wall beside his bed
To hang his pants on while he slept.

ODE TO PLEASURE

from the French of La Fontaine

PLEASURE, whom had we lacked from earliest hour,
To live or die had come to seem as one,
Of all creatures the sole magnet-stone,
How surely are we drawn by thy great power!
      Here, thou art mover of all things.
      For thee, for thy soft blandishings
      We fly to troubles and to harms.
      No captain is, nor man-at-arms,
Nor subject, minister, nor royalty,
      Who does not singly aim at thee.
We other nurslings, did not our labors bear
The fruits of fame, delicious to the ear,
And were this sound not pleasurably heard,
      Then should we rhyme a single word?
That which the world calls glory, and acclaims,
Which served as guerdon in the Olympic games,
Truly is none but thee, O divine Pleasure.
And shall the joys of sense not fill thy measure?
      For whom are Flora's gifts outlaid,
      The Sunset and Aurora made,
      Pomona and her tasty fare,
      Bacchus, soul of banquets rare,
      Waters, and forest-lands, and leas,
      The nourishers of reveries?
Wherefore so many arts, thy children all?
Why all these Chlorises, whose charms enthrall,
      Unless to make thy commerce thrive?
My meaning's innocent: whatever limit
      Rigor may for desire contrive,
      Nevertheless there's pleasure in it.

O Pleasure, Pleasure, in the former age
     Mistress of Hellas' gayest sage,
Pray scorn me not, come thence and stop with me;
     Idle thou shalt never be:
For games I love, and love, and every art,
Country, and town, and all; there's nought my mood
     May not convert to sovereign good,
Even to the gloom of melancholy heart.
Then come; and wouldst thou know, O sweetest Pleasure,
What measure of these goods must me befall?
Enough to fill a hundred years of leisure;
     For thirty were no good at all.

IN THE ELEGY SEASON

Haze, char, and the weather of All Souls':
A giant absence mopes upon the trees:
Leaves cast in casual potpourris
Whisper their scents from pits and cellar-holes.

Or brewed in gulleys, steeped in wells, they spend
In chilly steam their last aromas, yield
From shallow hells a revenance of field
And orchard air. And now the envious mind

Which could not hold the summer in my head
While bounded by that blazing circumstance
Parades these barrens in a golden trance,
Remembering the wealthy season dead,

And by an autumn inspiration makes
A summer all its own. Green boughs arise
Through all the boundless backward of the eyes,
And the soul bathes in warm conceptual lakes.

Less proud than this, my body leans an ear
Past cold and colder weather after wings'
Soft commotion, the sudden race of springs,
The goddess' tread heard on the dayward stair,

Longs for the brush of the freighted air, for smells
Of grass and cordial lilac, for the sight
Of green leaves building into the light
And azure water hoisting out of wells.

MARCHÉ AUX OISEAUX

Hundreds of birds are singing in the square.
Their minor voices fountaining in air
And constant as a fountain, lightly loud,
Do not drown out the burden of the crowd.

Far from his gold Sudan, the travailleur
Lends to the noise an intermittent chirr
Which to his hearers seems more joy than rage.
He batters softly at his wooden cage.

Here are the silver-bill, the orange-cheek,
The perroquet, the dainty coral-beak
Stacked in their cages; and around them move
The buyers in their termless hunt for love.

Here are the old, the ill, the imperial child;
The lonely people, desperate and mild;
The ugly; past these faces one can read
The tyranny of one outrageous need.

We love the small, said Burke. And if the small
Be not yet small enough, why then by Hell
We'll cramp it till it knows but how to feed,
And we'll provide the water and the seed.

JUGGLER

A ball will bounce, but less and less. It's not
A light-hearted thing, resents its own resilience.
Falling is what it loves, and the earth falls
So in our hearts from brilliance,
Settles and is forgot.
It takes a sky-blue juggler with five red balls

To shake our gravity up. Whee, in the air
The balls roll round, wheel on his wheeling hands,
Learning the ways of lightness, alter to spheres
Grazing his finger ends,
Cling to their courses there,
Swinging a small heaven about his ears.

But a heaven is easier made of nothing at all
Than the earth regained, and still and sole within
The spin of worlds, with a gesture sure and noble
He reels that heaven in,
Landing it ball by ball,
And trades it all for a broom, a plate, a table.

Oh, on his toe the table is turning, the broom's
Balancing up on his nose, and the plate whirls
On the tip of the broom! Damn, what a show, we cry:
The boys stamp, and the girls
Shriek, and the drum booms
And all comes down, and he bows and says good-bye.

If the juggler is tired now, if the broom stands
In the dust again, if the table starts to drop
Through the daily dark again, and though the plate
Lies flat on the table top,
For him we batter our hands
Who has won for once over the world's weight.

PARABLE

I read how Quixote in his random ride
Came to a crossing once, and lest he lose
The purity of chance, would not decide

Whither to fare, but wished his horse to choose.
For glory lay wherever he might turn.
His head was light with pride, his horse's shoes

Were heavy, and he headed for the barn.

THE GOOD SERVANT

Its piers less black for sunny smiles above,
My roadstead hand takes all the world for sea,
Or lifts to wingèd love
Its limed and leafless tree,
Or creeps into a glove
To greet mine enemy.

Angers the noble face
Would suffer unexpressed
This lackey in his place
Must serve to manifest,
Be mailed without as any carapace,
But soft within, where self to self is pressed.

Nights, when the head to other glory sets,
The hand turns turtle, lying like a lake
Where men with broken nets
Seek, for their master's sake,
All that that lord forgets
Because he would not wake.

Above the ceded plains
Visored volition stands
And sees my lands in chains
And ponders the commands
Of what were not impossible campaigns
If I would take my life into my hands.

PITY

The following day was overcast, each street
A slow canal to float him to the place
Where he'd let fall the dear and staring face,
A funnel toward the thin reproachful tweet.

All day the starved canary called him back
In newsboy's whistle, crying of a tire,
Squeak of a squeegee, sirens finding fire,
Until the nightfall packed his head in black,

And he went back and climbed the stairs again,
Stepping across her body, freed the bird,
Which left its cage and out the window whirred
As a bad thought out of a cracked brain.

THE SIRENS

I never knew the road
From which the whole earth didn't call away,
With wild birds rounding the hill crowns,
Haling out of the heart an old dismay,
Or the shore somewhere pounding its slow code,
Or low-lighted towns
Seeming to tell me, stay.

Lands I have never seen
And shall not see, loves I will not forget,
All I have missed, or slighted, or foregone
Call to me now. And weaken me. And yet
I would not walk a road without a scene.
I listen going on,
The richer for regret.

YEARS-END

Now winter downs the dying of the year,
And night is all a settlement of snow;
From the soft street the rooms of houses show
A gathered light, a shapen atmosphere,
Like frozen-over lakes whose ice is thin
And still allows some stirring down within.

I've known the wind by water banks to shake
The late leaves down, which frozen where they fell
And held in ice as dancers in a spell
Fluttered all winter long into a lake;
Graved on the dark in gestures of descent,
They seemed their own most perfect monument.

There was perfection in the death of ferns
Which laid their fragile cheeks against the stone
A million years. Great mammoths overthrown
Composedly have made their long sojourns,
Like palaces of patience, in the gray
And changeless lands of ice. And at Pompeii

The little dog lay curled and did not rise
But slept the deeper as the ashes rose
And found the people incomplete, and froze
The random hands, the loose unready eyes
Of men expecting yet another sun
To do the shapely thing they had not done.

These sudden ends of time must give us pause.
We fray into the future, rarely wrought
Save in the tapestries of afterthought.
More time, more time. Barrages of applause
Come muffled from a buried radio.
The New-year bells are wrangling with the snow.

23

THE PURITANS

Sidling upon the river, the white boat
Has volleyed with its cannon all the morning,
Shaken the shore towns like a Judgment warning,
Telling the palsied water its demand
That the crime come to the top again, and float,
That the sunk murder rise to the light and land.

Blam. In the noon's perfected brilliance burn
Brief blooms of flame, which soil away in smoke;
And down below, where slowed concussion broke
The umber stroll of waters, water-dust
Dreamily powders up, and serves to turn
The river surface to a cloudy rust.

Down from his bridge the river captain cries
To fire again. They make the cannon sound;
But none of them would wish the murder found,
Nor wish in other manner to atone
Than booming at their midnight crime, which lies
Rotting the river, weighted with a stone.

GRASSE: THE OLIVE TREES

for Marcelle and Ferdinand Springer

Here luxury's the common lot. The light
Lies on the rain-pocked rocks like yellow wool
And around the rocks the soil is rusty bright
From too much wealth of water, so that the grass
Mashes under the foot, and all is full
Of heat and juice and a heavy jammed excess.

Whatever moves moves with the slow complete
Gestures of statuary. Flower smells
Are set in the golden day, and shelled in heat,
Pine and columnar cypress stand. The palm
Sinks its combs in the sky. This whole South swells
To a soft rigor, a rich and crowded calm.

Only the olive contradicts. My eye,
Traveling slopes of rust and green, arrests
And rests from plenitude where olives lie
Like clouds of doubt against the earth's array.
Their faint disheveled foliage divests
The sunlight of its color and its sway.

Not that the olive spurns the sun; its leaves
Scatter and point to every part of the sky,
Like famished fingers waving. Brilliance weaves
And sombers down among them, and among
The anxious silver branches, down to the dry
And twisted trunk, by rooted hunger wrung.

Even when seen from near, the olive shows
A hue of far away. Perhaps for this
The dove brought olive back, a tree which grows
Unearthly pale, which ever dims and dries,
And whose great thirst, exceeding all excess,
Teaches the South it is not paradise.

THE AVOWAL

from the French of Villiers de l'Isle Adam

I have lost the wood, the heath,
Fresh Aprils long gone by. . . .
Give me your lips: their breath
Shall be the forest's sigh.

I have lost the sullen Sea,
Its glooms, its echoed caves;
Speak only: it shall be
The murmur of the waves.

By royal grief oppressed
I dream of a vanished light. . . .
Hold me: in that pale breast
Shall be the calm of night.

THE GIFTS

from the French of Villiers de l'Isle Adam

If you speak to me, some night,
Of my sick heart's secret bale,
To ease you I'll recite
An ancient ballad-tale.

Or if you speak of pain
And hopes long fallen due,
I shall but gather then
The dew-filled rose for you.

If, like the flower which grows
In the exile soil of graves,
You beg to share my woes . . .
I'll bring you a gift of doves.

FIVE WOMEN BATHING IN MOONLIGHT

When night believes itself alone
It is most natural, conceals
No artifice. The open moon
With webs in sky and water wields

The slightest wave. This vision yields
To a cool accord of semblance, land
Leasing each wave the palest peals
Of bright apparent notes of sand.

The bathers whitely come and stand.
Water diffuses them, their hair
Like seaweed slurs the shoulders, and
Their voices in the moonstrung air

Go plucked of words. Now wading where
The moon's misprision salves them in-
To silver, they are unaware
How lost they are when they begin

To mix with water, making then
Gestures of blithe obedience,
As five Danilovas within
The soft compulsions of their dance.

THE TERRACE

De la vaporisation et de la centralisation du Moi. *Tout est là.*

De la vaporisation et de la centralisation du Moi. *Tout est là.*
                                                    —BAUDELAIRE

We ate with steeps of sky about our shoulders,
High up a mountainside,
On a terrace like a raft roving
Seas of view.

The tablecloth was green, and blurred away
Toward verdure far and wide,
And all the country came to be
Our table too.

We drank in tilted glasses of rosé
From tinted peaks of snow,
Tasting the frothy mist, and freshest
Fathoms of air.

Women were washing linens in a stream
Deep down below,
The sound of water over their knuckles
A sauce rare.

Imminent towns whose weatherbeaten walls
Looked like the finest cheese
Bowled us enormous melons from their
Tolling towers.

Mixt into all the day we heard the spice
Of many tangy bees
Eddying through the miles-deep
Salad of flowers.

When we were done we had our hunger still;
We dipped our cups in light;

29

We caught the fine-spun shade of clouds
In spoon and plate;

Drunk with imagined breathing, we inhaled
The dancing smell of height;
We fished for the bark of a dog, the squeak
Of a pasture gate.

But for all our benedictions and our gay
Readily said graces,
The evening stole our provender and
Left us there,

And darkness filled the specious space, and fell
Betwixt our silent faces,
Pressing against our eyes its absent
Fathomless stare.

Out in the dark we felt the real mountains
Hulking in proper might,
And we felt the edge of the black wind's
Regardless cleave,

And we knew we had eaten not the manna of heaven
But our own reflected light,
And we were the only part of the night that we
Couldn't believe.

A PROBLEM FROM MILTON

In Eden palm and open-handed pine
Displayed to God and man their flat perfection.
Carefully coiled, the regulation vine
Submitted to our general sire's inspection.

And yet the streams in mazy error went;
Powdery flowers a potent odor gave;
The trees, on second thoughts, were lushly blent
And swashed forever like a piling wave.

The builded comber like a hurdling horse
Achieves the rocks. With wild informal roar
The spray upholds its freedom and its force,
But leaves the limpet and the whelk ashore.

In spirals of the whelk's eternal shell
The mind of Swedenborg to heaven flew,
But found it such a mathematic hell
That Emerson was damned if it would do.

Poor Adam, deviled by your energy,
What power egged you on to feed your brains?
Envy the gorgeous gallops of the sea,
Whose horses never know their lunar reins.

A GLANCE FROM THE BRIDGE

Letting the eye descend from reeking stack
And black façade to where the river goes,
You see the freeze has started in to crack
(As if the city squeezed it in a vice),
And here and there the limbering water shows,
And gulls colonial on the sullied ice.

Some rise and braid their glidings, white and spare,
Or sweep the hemmed-in river up and down,
Making a litheness in the barriered air,
And through the town the freshening water swirls
As if an ancient whore undid her gown
And showed a body almost like a girl's.

CLEARNESS

There is a poignancy in all things clear,
In the stare of the deer, in the ring of a hammer in the morning.
Seeing a bucket of perfectly lucid water
We fall to imagining prodigious honesties.

And feel so when the snow for all its softness
Tumbles in adamant forms, turning and turning
Its perfect faces, littering on our sight
The heirs and types of timeless dynasties.

In pine-woods once that huge precision of leaves
Amazed my eyes and closed them down a dream.
I lost to mind the usual southern river,
Mud, mist, the plushy sound of the oar,

And pondering north through lifted veils of gulls,
Through sharpening calls, and blue clearings of steam,
I came and anchored by a fabulous town
Immaculate, high, and never found before.

This was the town of my mind's exacted vision
Where truths fell from the bells like a jackpot of dimes,
And the people's voices, carrying over the water,
Sang in the ear as clear and sweet as birds.

But this was Thulë of the mind's worst vanity;
Nor could I tell the burden of those clear chimes;
And the fog fell, and the stainless voices faded;
I had not understood their lovely words.

*

The asterisk
Says look below, as a star
We prize for its being far
And longing ask
For some release,
Joins to a dog or a bear,
A dipper, a tipping chair.
They give us peace
These downward looks
Of stars, the way they note
The birth of gods, and dote
On seaward brooks.
Some of the sea's
Stars are alive, I've seen
Them figure the white-green
Ocean frieze;
And I've known
The sea so rich and black
It gave the starlight back
Brighter. It shone
As if the high
Vault were its glass, and thus
It is. It's up to us
To gloss the sky.

GAMES TWO

:

From barren coldness birds
Go squadroned South;
So from the hollow mouth
The way of words
Is East. When written down
As here, they file
In broken bands awhile,
But never noun
Found what it named; for lame,
Lost, though they burn
For the East, all words must turn
Back where they came
From, back to their old
Capital. Still,
As pilgrims on a hill
Fallen, behold
With failing eyes from far
The desired city,
Silence will take pity
On words. There are
Pauses where words must wait,
Spaces in speech
Which stop and calm it, and each
Is like a gate:

Past which creation lies
In morning sun,
Where word with world is one
And nothing dies.

The land was overmuch like scenery,
The flowers attentive, the grass too garrulous green;
In the lake like a dropped kerchief could be seen
The lark's reflection after the lark was gone;
The Roman road lay paved too shiningly
For a road so many men had traveled on.

Also the people were strange, were strangely warm.
The king recalled the father of his guest,
The queen brought mead in a studded cup, the rest
Were kind, but in all was a vagueness and a strain,
Because they lived in a land of daily harm.
And they said the same things again and again.

It was a childish country; and a child,
Grown monstrous, so besieged them in the night
That all their daytimes were a dream of fright
That it would come and own them to the bone.
The hero, to his battle reconciled,
Promised to meet that monster all alone.

So then the people wandered to their sleep
And left him standing in the echoed hall.
They heard the rafters rattle fit to fall, .
The child departing with a broken groan,
And found their champion in a rest so deep
His head lay harder sealed than any stone.

The land was overmuch like scenery,
The lake gave up the lark, but now its song
Fell to no ear, the flowers too were wrong,
The day was fresh and pale and swiftly old,

The night put out no smiles upon the sea;
And the people were strange, the people strangely cold.

They gave him horse and harness, helmet and mail,
A jeweled shield, an ancient battle-sword,
Such gifts as are the hero's hard reward
And bid him do again what he has done.
These things he stowed beneath his parting sail,
And wept that he could share them with no son.

He died in his own country a kinless king,
A name heavy with deeds, and mourned as one
Will mourn for the frozen year when it is done.
They buried him next the sea on a thrust of land:
Twelve men rode round his barrow all in a ring,
Singing of him what they could understand.

STILL, CITIZEN SPARROW

Still, citizen sparrow, this vulture which you call
Unnatural, let him but lumber again to air
Over the rotten office, let him bear
The carrion ballast up, and at the tall

Tip of the sky lie cruising. Then you'll see
That no more beautiful bird is in heaven's height,
No wider more placid wings, no watchfuller flight;
He shoulders nature there, the frightfully free,

The naked-headed one. Pardon him, you
Who dart in the orchard aisles, for it is he
Devours death, mocks mutability,
Has heart to make an end, keeps nature new.

Thinking of Noah, childheart, try to forget
How for so many bedlam hours his saw
Soured the song of birds with its wheezy gnaw,
And the slam of his hammer all the day beset

The people's ears. Forget that he could bear
To see the towns like coral under the keel,
And the fields so dismal deep. Try rather to feel
How high and weary it was, on the waters where

He rocked his only world, and everyone's.
Forgive the hero, you who would have died
Gladly with all you knew; he rode that tide
To Ararat; all men are Noah's sons.

WELLFLEET: THE HOUSE

Roof overwoven by a soft tussle of leaves,
The walls awave with sumac shadow, lilac
Lofts and falls in the yard, and the house believes
It's guarded, garlanded in a former while.

Here one cannot intrude, the stillness being
Lichenlike grown, a coating of quietudes;
The portraits dream themselves, they are done with seeing;
Rocker and teacart balance in iron moods.

Yet for the transient here is no offense,
Because at certain hours a wallowed light
Floods at the seaside windows, vague, intense,
And lays on all within a mending blight,

Making the kitchen silver blindly gleam,
The yellow floorboards swim, the dazzled clock
Boom with a buoy sound, the chambers seem
Alluvial as that champed and glittering rock

The sea strokes up to fashion dune and beach
In strew by strew, and year by hundred years.
One is at home here. Nowhere in ocean's reach
Can time have any foreignness or fears.

THE DEATH OF A TOAD

A toad the power mower caught,
Chewed and clipped of a leg, with a hobbling hop has got
  To the garden verge, and sanctuaried him
  Under the cineraria leaves, in the shade
    Of the ashen heartshaped leaves, in a dim,
      Low, and a final glade.

The rare original heartsblood goes,
Spends on the earthen hide, in the folds and wizenings, flows
  In the gutters of the banked and staring eyes. He lies
  As still as if he would return to stone,
    And soundlessly attending, dies
      Toward some deep monotone,

Toward misted and ebullient seas
And cooling shores, toward lost Amphibia's emperies.
  Day dwindles, drowning, and at length is gone
  In the wide and antique eyes, which still appear
    To watch, across the castrate lawn,
      The haggard daylight steer.

DRIFTWOOD

In greenwoods once these relics must have known
A rapt, gradual growing,
That are cast here like slag of the old
Engine of grief;

Must have affirmed in annual increase
Their close selves, knowing
Their own nature only, and that
Bringing to leaf.

Say, for the seven cities or a war
Their solitude was taken,
They into masts shaven, or milled into
Oar and plank;

Afterward sailing long and to lost ends,
By groundless water shaken,
Well they availed their vessels till they
Smashed or sank.

Then on the great generality of waters
Floated their singleness,
And in all that deep subsumption they were
Never dissolved;

But shaped and flowingly fretted by the waves'
Ever surpassing stress,
With the gnarled swerve and tangle of tides
Finely involved.

Brought in the end where breakers dump and slew
On the glass verge of the land,

Silver they rang to the stones when the sea
Flung them and turned.

Curious crowns and scepters they look to me
Here on the gold sand,
Warped, wry, but having the beauty of
Excellence earned.

In a time of continual dry abdications
And of damp complicities,
They are fit to be taken for signs, these emblems
Royally sane,

Which have ridden to homeless wreck, and long revolved
In the lathe of all the seas,
But have saved in spite of it all their dense
Ingenerate grain.

A COURTYARD THAW

The sun was strong enough today
To climb the wall and loose the courtyard trees
(For two short hours, anyway)
From hardship of the January freeze.

Their icy cerements decayed
To silken moistures, which began to slip
In glints and spangles down, and made
On every twig a bauble at the tip.

No blossom, leaf or basking fruit
Showed ever such pure passion for the sun
As these cold drops that knew no root
Yet filled with light and swelled and one by one

(Or showered by a wingbeat, sown
From windbent branches in arpeggios)
Let go and took their shinings down
And brought their brittle season to a close.

O false gemmation! Flashy fall!
The eye is pleased when nature stoops to art,
Staging within a courtyard wall
Such twinkling scenes. But puzzling to the heart,

This spring was neither fierce nor gay;
This summary autumn fell without a tear:
No tinkling music-box can play
The slow, deep-grounded masses of the year.

LAMENT

Nashe's old queens who bartered young and fair
Their light tiaras for such ponderous stones:
Of them I'd think, how sunlit still their hair,
And fine as airship frames their balanced bones.

It is, I say, a most material loss.
Kept spirit is corporate; doubly the thought of you,
As air fills air, or waves together toss,
Out of my wishes and your being grew.

Water and air: such unclenched stuff can last,
But rarest things are visible and firm;
Grace falls the fastest from our failing past,
And I lament for grace's early term,

For casual dances that your body knows,
Whose spirit only sense can understand,
For times when spirit, doomed and single, flows
Into the speeches of your eye and hand.

FLUMEN TENEBRARUM

This night's colossal quiet, in heaven crowned
Immoveable, at earth is slippered swift
With shore grasses' wind-ushering sound,
With the river's folding drift,

With our own vanishing voices as we go
By the stream side, watching our shadows dangled
Down the bank to the flood, trailed in the flow
And all in stars entangled.

There is the hunter hulking up the night
Who waded once the wildest of our seas,
With foiled eyes marking the still flight
Of the faint Pleiades.

And here are we, who hold each other now
So nearly, that our welded shadows seem,
There where they fall away, a ghostly prow
Steering into the stream.

As if to kiss were someway to embark;
As if to love were partly to be spent,
And send of us a hostage to the dark.
If so, I am content,

And would not have my lively longing freeze,
Nor your delays, in figures of the sky,
Since none outlasts the stream, and even these
Must come to life and die.

The hunter shall be tumbled in this tide,
Worse stricken than by Dian's steepest arrow,

And all his fire shall gutter out beside
This old embarcadero;

Those nymphs, so long preserved, at last be lost,
Be borne again along this blackening race,
And with their lover swept away, and tossed
In scintillant embrace.

FROM THE LOOKOUT ROCK

Oh wind I hear you faltering,
In long cessation dying down,
Failing the osprey's pillowed wing,
Franchising all the peaceful graves,
The lifted waters letting fall
And all the flags of every town,
Because your slackened voices crawl
To bass finales in their caves.

The parching stones along the shore
Hastily sip the listless waves,
In doubt the sea will pour them more
When lull has loitered into calm;
A tenantry of jays in swarm
Issues rebellious from the leaves
And rising makes a patch of storm
Above the quiet of their elm.

Good-bye the roving of the land:
The tumbling weed of all the West
Engraves its shadow on the sand.
Haphazard stand the weather-vanes,
Unrocked the cradles of the vales,
The ropes are loose of every mast,
Appalled are all the sagging sails
And overhushed the ocean-lanes.

The fishers for Atlantis see
A stillness on the ocean grow
Deeper than that of history.
Venturers to the pole turn round
And watch the southward cities fill
With space as barren as their snow.

The cities' voices fall and still
To hear the wide retreat of sound.

I from this rock espy a gull
Riding the raveled last of air
Who folds his wings, and tips to fall
Beside the pillar of the sun.
(The drumhead bay is like a lake,
A great and waiting skyward stare.)
The shoreline gives a timbrel shake:
Our last Icarian moment, done.

Gods of the wind, return again,
For this was not the peace we prayed;
Intone again your burdened strain,
And weave the world to harmony,
Voyage the seed along the breeze,
Reviving all your former trade,
Restore the lilting of the trees
And massive dances of the sea.

TO AN AMERICAN POET JUST DEAD

In the *Boston Sunday Herald* just three lines
Of no-point type for you who used to sing
The praises of imaginary wines,
And died, or so I'm told, of the real thing.

Also gone, but a lot less forgotten,
Are an eminent cut-rate druggist, a lover of Giving,
A lender, and various brokers: gone from this rotten
Taxable world to a higher standard of living.

It is out in the comfy suburbs I read you are dead,
And the soupy summer is settling, full of the yawns
Of Sunday fathers loitering late in bed,
And the ssshh of sprays on all the little lawns.

Will the sprays weep wide for you their chaplet tears?
For you will the deep-freeze units melt and mourn?
For you will Studebakers shred their gears
And sound from each garage a muted horn?

They won't. In summer sunk and stupefied
The suburbs deepen in their sleep of death.
And though they sleep the sounder since you died
It's just as well that now you save your breath.

GIACOMETTI

Rock insults us, hard and so boldly browed
Its scorn needs not to focus, and with fists
Which still unstirring strike:
Collected it resists
Until its buried glare begets a like
Anger in us, and finds our hardness. Proud,

Then, and armed, and with a patient rage
We carve cliff, shear stone to blocks,
And down to the image of man
Batter and shape the rock's
Fierce composure, closing its veins within
That outside man, itself its captive cage.

So we can baffle rock, and in our will
Can clothe and keep it. But if our will, though locked
In stone it clutches, change,
Then are we much worse mocked
Than cliffs can do: then we ourselves are strange
To what we were, which lowers on us still.

High in the air those habitants of stone
Look heavenward, lean to a thought, or stride
Toward some concluded war,
While we on every side,
Random as shells the sea drops down ashore,
Are walking, walking, many and alone.

What stony shape could hold us now, what hard
Bent can we bulk in air, where shall our feet
Come to a common stand?
Follow along this street

(Where rock recovers carven eye and hand),
Open the gate, and cross the narrow yard

And look where Giacometti in a room
Dim as a cave of the sea, has built the man
We are, and made him walk:
Towering like a thin
Coral, out of a reef of plaster chalk,
This is the single form we can assume.

We are this man unspeakably alone
Yet stripped of the singular utterly, shaved and scraped
Of all but being there,
Whose fullness is escaped
Like a burst balloon's: no nakedness so bare
As flesh gone in inquiring of the bone.

He is pruned of every gesture, saving only
The habit of coming and going. Every pace
Shuffles a million feet.
The faces in this face
Are all forgotten faces of the street
Gathered to one anonymous and lonely.

No prince and no Leviathan, he is made
Of infinite farewells. Oh never more
Diminished, nonetheless
Embodied here, we are
This starless walker, one who cannot guess
His will, his keel his nose's bony blade.

And volumes hover round like future shades
This least of man, in whom we join and take

A pilgrim's step behind,
And in whose guise we make
Our grim departures now, walking to find
What railleries of rock, what palisades?

HE WAS

a brown old man with a green thumb:
I can remember the screak on stones of his hoe,
The chug, choke, and high madrigal wheeze
Of the spray-cart bumping below
The sputtery leaves of the apple trees,
But he was all but dumb

Who filled some quarter of the day with sound
All of my childhood long. For all I heard
Of all his labors, I can now recall
Never a single word
Until he went in the dead of fall
To the drowsy underground,

Having planted a young orchard with so great care
In that last year that none was lost, and May
Aroused them all, the leaves saying the land's
Praise for the livening clay,
And the found voice of his buried hands
Rose in the sparrowy air.

A SIMILE FOR HER SMILE

Your smiling, or the hope, the thought of it,
Makes in my mind such pause and abrupt ease
As when the highway bridgegates fall,
Balking the hasty traffic, which must sit
On each side massed and staring, while
Deliberately the drawbridge starts to rise:

Then horns are hushed, the oilsmoke rarefies,
Above the idling motors one can tell
The packet's smooth approach, the slip,
Slip of the silken river past the sides,
The ringing of clear bells, the dip
And slow cascading of the paddle wheel.

CEREMONY

A striped blouse in a clearing by Bazille
Is, you may say, a patroness of boughs
Too queenly kind toward nature to be kin.
But ceremony never did conceal,
Save to the silly eye, which all allows,
How much we are the woods we wander in.

Let her be some Sabrina fresh from stream,
Lucent as shallows slowed by wading sun,
Bedded on fern, the flowers' cynosure:
Then nymph and wood must nod and strive to dream
That she is airy earth, the trees, undone,
Must ape her languor natural and pure.

Ho-hum. I am for wit and wakefulness,
And love this feigning lady by Bazille.
What's lightly hid is deepest understood,
And when with social smile and formal dress
She teaches leaves to curtsey and quadrille,
I think there are most tigers in the wood.

Date Due

DEC 18 '64		
OCT 1 1 1968		
GB	PRINTED	IN U. S. A.